happy brides
survival guide

happy bride's
survival guide

Leigh Crandall

RYLAND
PETERS
& SMALL
LONDON NEW YORK

Senior designer Sonya Nathoo
Commissioning editor Annabel Morgan
Picture researcher Emily Westlake
Production Gordana Simakovic
Art director Leslie Harrington
Publishing director Alison Starling

First published in the UK in 2010
by Ryland Peters & Small
20–21 Jockey's Fields
London WC1R 4BW

and in the US in 2010
by Ryland Peters & Small
519 Broadway, Fifth Floor
New York, NY 10012

www.rylandpeters.com
Text, design and photographs
© Ryland Peters & Small 2010

10 9 8 7 6 5 4 3 2 1

ISBN 978-1-84597-946-1

A CIP record for this book is available
from the British Library.

Printed and bound in China

Contents

Introduction

First of all, many congratulations! If you're reading this book, then you're probably newly engaged and starting to think about what your wedding might be like. It's a very exciting time and, while wedding planning is bound to be a little stressful, hopefully the whole process of putting your wedding celebration together will be a happy and rewarding experience.

One of the best things about weddings today is that there really aren't any hard-and-fast rules that you have to adhere to. Your wedding can be anything you want it to be, and it will be a success just so long as you and your fiancé stay true to yourselves. Sure, weddings can be expensive, but you truly don't have to break the bank to throw a gorgeous, memorable celebration—many of the loveliest weddings are also the simplest.

This little book is intended to give you an overview of the planning process, and offer advice and information to get you started. Hopefully, you'll find it a useful tool in making your wedding everything you want it to be!

getting started

Wedding planning timeline

Up to a year before

❋ Determine the approximate number of guests you want to invite

❋ Set a budget

❋ Select the wedding party

❋ Decide at what time of the year you want to get married

12 to 9 months before

❋ Interview wedding planners and hire one if you decide you want to do so

❋ Reserve your ceremony and reception venues

❋ Book ceremony officiant

❋ Meet with and book photographer, videographer, band or DJ, and florist

❋ Go for tastings with potential caterers

❋ Register for your gift list

8 to 7 months before

❋ Research hotels for your guests to stay at, and book a block of rooms if possible

❋ Finalize the guest list

❋ Find and order your wedding gown and veil

❋ Send out save-the-date cards

6 months before

❋ Create a wedding website if you intend to have one

❋ Shop for and order the bridesmaid dresses

5 months before

❋ Order the invitations

❋ Book the rehearsal dinner venue

❋ Think about what you might want your ceremony to be like and discuss it with your officiant; book the ceremony musicians if you intend to have them

❋ Schedule hair and makeup trials and book hair and makeup artists

❋ Go on tastings and book a wedding cake designer

4 months before

❋ Order or make the order of service/ceremony programs, menu cards, and table cards

❋ Arrange the transportation for the wedding party

❋ Book the honeymoon

❋ Decide on any flower girl/ring bearer outfits and order them if necessary

3 months before

※ Buy the wedding rings

※ Finalize the ceremony readings and music

※ Finalize the menu, the cake, and the floral details

※ Create a "day of wedding" timeline (see pages 54–55). Send copies of this to your wedding planner and your vendors

※ Schedule your first wedding gown fitting

※ Buy the attendants' gifts

2 months before

※ Mail the invitations

※ Meet with your photographer to discuss the shots you want. Create a list of important moments and people you want photographed

※ Submit your wedding announcement to the newspaper

1 month before

※ Review your playlist with the band or DJ

※ Apply for marriage license

※ Complete gown fittings

2 weeks before

※ Confirm the times and plan with all your vendors

※ Have your hair cut and colored (if you're planning to)

※ Send the final guest count to your caterer so they have exact numbers

※ Confirm number of guests with the rehearsal dinner venue

※ Do any last-minute shopping for your honeymoon

Week of

※ Prepare envelopes containing payments and tips for the vendors (for distribution on the day)

※ Make welcome baskets and deliver to hotels where out-of-town guests will be staying

※ Finalize the seating chart and write the place cards

※ Have a manicure and pedicure

※ Pack for your honeymoon

Setting your budget

The first step in the planning process is to determine your budget.

It's important that you and your fiancé, as well as both sets of parents (if they're going to contribute), are all on the same page as far as financing the celebration goes.

Discuss the sort of wedding you imagine having with your husband-to-be. It's important that the two of you share a general idea of what you want. Figure out what you can contribute to the budget as a couple, then talk your ideas over with your parents. If they intend to foot part (or any, or all) of the bill, be sure you understand their expectations and accept their limits.

Once you have a sum in mind, take advantage of the numerous online wedding budget planners available to allot funds for specific purposes. Decide what's most important to you—a special venue, haute cuisine, or an incredible photographer—

and find out what it will cost. Then adjust the figures accordingly. Think about ways you can save (cutting down your guest list, or getting married off-season or on a day other than Saturday, for example) and don't be afraid to bargain with vendors. Ask crafty friends and family to donate their talents. Lastly, identify any areas where you can be flexible. If you have your heart set on a band that's a bit pricey, maybe you could skip sending save-the-date cards, or arrange the table flowers yourself.

In the end, it's important that you stick to your budget. It's easy to get swept up in all of the possibilities, but you won't enjoy your wedding as much if you feel stressed or guilty about the cost. Make the most with what you have, and then embrace your day—if you and your groom love it, then your guests will, too.

Choosing your venue

The wedding venue sets the tone for your entire celebration, so clearly it's essential you pick somewhere that you both love.

While hunting for your reception venue, it's important to keep both your budget and your number of guests in mind. Think about the time of year you plan to get married, and imagine what the site will look like then. Be sure to pick somewhere that works with your overall vision of your big day. When you're looking, consider not only event spaces and hotels, but also museums, historical sites, even your own back yard. And don't knock a place before you've seen it—with a little creativity, even the most ordinary spaces can be transformed into something amazing.

Questions to ask when you're looking around a potential venue:

※ What are the rental fees, and what exactly is included?

※ What's the parking situation, and what are the facilities like?

※ If you're planning an outdoor celebration, is there a "Plan B" space that will work as backup if it rains?

※ Are there any noise restrictions, and what time are parties allowed to begin and end?

※ Are outside caterers allowed?

※ What are the cancellation and payment policies?

Themes and decorations

One of the easiest ways to create a cohesive look for your wedding is to choose a color scheme that can be repeated throughout your celebration, from the save-the-date cards to the reception flowers.

Establishing a wedding color scheme certainly doesn't mean that absolutely everything has to be "matchy-matchy," but keeping your wedding elements within a pre-determined palette will certainly give your celebration a more unified and elegant look. When it comes to choosing your scheme, bear in mind the time of year, the setting, and the level of formality you want your celebration to have.

Another way to tie the different wedding elements together is to incorporate a decorative motif or theme. Look to your location for ideas—maybe there's a legendary story attached to the venue that inspires your choice of table names, or a gorgeous stand-out architectural detail that will work perfectly as a typographic motif on the invitations.

You could also draw inspiration from you and your fiancé's shared history. Your favorite date spot; movies or books that you both love; your beloved pet; the trips you've taken together; even your jobs or the décor of your apartment can provide the starting point for concepts that can be reflected in the table settings, the wedding cake, or the wedding favors.

Color schemes that work well:

- pale peach, apricot, cream, and khaki

- rose, periwinkle, lavender, and sage

- smoke, pale yellow, and white

- brown, butter yellow, and cornflower blue

- silver, black, and white

Your vendors

Wedding vendors rely on word of mouth for the majority of their business and for good reason: if you're getting married in an area where your friends and family live, their personal recommendations are the easiest way to track down the best people to work with.

If you don't have recommendations to go on, a little research will be required. Check out local wedding magazines and websites in the area your wedding is being held. Look at different websites to find vendors whose work appeals. Meet with people who have an aesthetic similar to that of the wedding you want. Don't try and fit a square peg into a round hole—if a florist is known for avant-garde arrangements and you're looking for something at the more traditional end of the spectrum, their skill set probably isn't going to be a good match. If you and a vendor hit it off well, ask if they have any recommendations—they attend weddings on a weekly basis and may have helpful suggestions for other people you might enjoy working with.

Before you meet with the florist, caterer, or photographer, it's helpful to make a list of words to describe the mood of the wedding you want. This will come in very handy when you're discussing concepts. And, since everyone's notion of "romantic" can be different, you could keep an inspiration folder to show vendors. This should include images of other weddings you've seen and liked, but can also contain fashion images, magazine clippings, fabric swatches, and anything else that can help communicate the vibe of your wedding to vendors.

Words to try:

- Vintage
- Retro
- Old-fashioned
- Modern
- Rustic
- Glamorous
- Romantic
- Casual
- Sweet
- Minimal
- Whimsical
- Playful
- Country
- Homespun

Things and places to inspire you:

- Movies you love
- The theater and opera
- Art museums
- Design blogs
- Magazines
- Your favorite shops
- Book illustrations
- Advertisements
- Your dream vacation spot

Registering for a wedding gift list

Wedding registries or gift lists are pretty standard nowadays. They're an easy way to pick the gifts you want, and are helpful to your family and friends, who want to get you a present they know you'll appreciate.

A good rule of thumb is to register with two or three different suppliers (but certainly not more than four) and to include one national chain—this makes life easier for those guests who prefer not to shop online.

Pick a wide variety of gifts that range in price, and think carefully about what you actually need—that crystal bowl may look pretty, but functionless items tend to sit around unopened. Consider your lifestyle and choose gifts that fit with it—if you're both very outdoorsy and don't much enjoy cooking, a new tent will likely be a better-used gift than a new wok or state-of-the-art food processor. Don't worry about choosing unconventional items. Ultimately, your guests just want to get you a gift you'll really like and appreciate.

If you and your fiancé already live together, you may find that you've already acquired most of the traditional wedding gifts, such as china, glassware, and household linen. If this is the case, you may want to go for an alternative gift list. Some couples are now opting to ask guests to contribute to their honeymoon (www.travelersjoy.com or www.buy-our-honeymoon) or choosing wine wedding lists to start building a cellar (check out www.bottlenotes.com or www.thewineweddinglist.co.uk).

Another increasingly popular choice is to simply ask your guests to make charitable donations instead of buying you a gift (see websites such as www.idofoundation.org, www.weddinglistgiving.com, or www.justgiving.com).

Q & A

How should I let my guests know where I'm registered?

This mostly happens via word of mouth—your family will probably ask your parents and your friends may ask you directly as well. It's also fine to list the shops you're registered at on your wedding website, if you've created one. Lastly, the names of these shops may be included by the host/hostess of your wedding shower on an insert enclosed with the shower invitation.

It is not acceptable to put gift registry information on your save-the-date cards or wedding invitations. While giving presents is a traditional gesture, guests should not be made to feel it's required of them if they plan to attend your wedding.

My fiancé's parents are divorced and they both want to contribute to the wedding. What's a good way to discuss finances with them?

If parents are separated and both want to contribute, one easy way to make sure they feel they've contributed equally is to come up with a set amount that each can donate toward the wedding. If divorced parents cannot contribute equal amounts, another easy solution is to suggest that each parent chooses one certain aspect of the celebration to pay for, depending on their budget. For example, one parent could cover the cost of the photographer or flowers, while the other could cover the cost of catering the event.

Do I have to provide my vendors with food at the reception?

If your wedding professionals are expecting to eat during your reception, this fact is likely to have been included in the contract you've signed with them. However, even if it isn't a part of the contract, it's a nice gesture to offer your photographer, videographer, wedding planner, and the DJ or members of the band some sustenance, since they'll be working hard for at least four or five hours.

Vendors don't need the same menu options as your guests; just something to curb their hunger. Ask your caterer about preparing a less expensive meal to serve them. If your vendors do plan to break for dinner, be sure you or your planner has discussed the timing of their break—you don't want it to overlap with any major wedding moments you'll need them for.

wedding style

Finding your gown

Your wedding gown search should be fun and exciting, and certainly one of the most special shopping experiences of your life.

There are a wide variety of bridal stores ranging from the quaint boutique, to the national department store chain, to the discount warehouse. To help you choose which shops to visit, you should:

※ ask for friends' recommendations
※ research bridal designers you like and find out which stores carry them
※ consider the shopping environment you're most likely to enjoy. If you like a lot of hands-on service, you may prefer a small salon. If you want to hunt the racks yourself, a larger store might be right for you.

Once you've narrowed down which stores you want to visit, the next step is making an appointment to go in and look at their gowns. If you want to visit several different stores, remember you don't have to hit all of them in a day. Start with the one or two you're most excited about. And don't worry if you don't find a dress you love right away (or if you find several you adore)—you can go back as many times as you need to.

To avoid feeling rushed into having to make a decision, start dress-shopping at least nine months before your wedding day, as some custom-ordered/made-to-measure gowns take several months to create. You'll want your dress to arrive about two months before the wedding, to allow for fittings.

Here are some other thoughts to keep in mind for a happy shopping experience:
※ Keep the venue and season of your wedding in mind—your gown should fit the look of your location, and you'll want to pick a fabric that will be comfortable depending on the time of the year.

※ Don't take your whole wedding party out shopping. Choose one or two friends or family members whose opinion you trust and who you have fun with. Remember, gown-shopping should be exciting, not stressful! Make a day of it and take your fellow shoppers out to lunch or dinner as a thank you.

※ Know what suits you. Picture the outfits you already own and feel good in. Consider the necklines, silhouettes and materials of these pieces—a wedding gown with similar features might work well for you.

※ Go armed with ideas. Bring pictures of dresses you like or any other elements (your venue, flowers, etc.) that fit with the vibe of the wedding to show the salesperson. Once she understands the look you're trying to create, she will be able to make dress suggestions that will suit the feel of your wedding. Trust the salesperson to know what size dress to order (wedding gown sizes vary widely by brand) and ask for their recommendations on gown cleaning services—they do this for a living, after all.

※ Arrive feeling confident. You don't have to be dressed for a night on the town, but this is a special occasion and you'll be more likely to get excited about dresses if you look your best. Wear clothes that are easy to slip in and out of. You'll also want to wear nude-colored underwear and a strapless bra.

※ Know your dress budget and ask that the salesperson show you gowns within that price range. If you fall in love with a dress that's a bit more than you'd planned to spend, it's time to bargain! It's worth asking if any adjustments to the material or embellishments of a gown can be made to lower the overall cost. If there's no room for negotiation on the dress price, it might be worth asking if the store is able to lower the cost of gown alterations or throw in some hair accessories or a pair of shoes for free. You may also want to ask about sample sales, when gowns that have been tried on previously are sold at a discount.

※ Once you have finally decided on your wedding dress and settled on a price, be

prepared to put down a 50 percent deposit when you place your order.

※ Finally, trust your instincts and pick the dress you feel most beautiful in!

Accessories, hair, and makeup

Your wedding day accessories offer the perfect opportunity to integrate the elements of that old wedding rhyme "something old, something new, something borrowed, something blue."

In keeping with tradition, you might:
※ borrow your grandmother's pearls to wear during the ceremony
※ wear your mother's wedding veil
※ have some lace from a family member's gown made into a handkerchief to carry with you, or somehow incorporate it into your bridal bouquet
※ refashion a relative's gown into a modern version that you can wear

Since most brides wear their wedding gown for the entire day, some change their accessories to take the look from day to evening. For example, you might wear a veil and simple, elegant earrings (pearl or diamond studs) for the ceremony, then change to a sparkling hair accessory or glamorous baubles for the reception.

Your shoes are a great place to add interest—an unexpected pop of blue or pink below your dress will look great in photographs. Plus, you're likely to get more use out of a gorgeous nonwhite pair of pumps. Purchase your shoes at least two months before the wedding, since you'll need to bring them to gown fittings and have a little time to break them in.

For your hair and makeup, opt for a dressier version of your normal look. Go for a trial or two with hair and makeup artists, and bring photos of looks you like. Consider what hairstyles will work best with your gown, and bring any hair accessories you plan to wear to your trial run, so you and your hairdresser can experiment with styles that will show them off best.

Dressing your bridesmaids

As with your gown, consider the wedding's formality and season when deciding upon bridesmaid dresses. These garments will appear in your wedding pictures, so choose carefully.

When it's time to shop, it's easiest to take along just one or two of your bridesmaids whose taste you really trust, rather than the entire group. Ultimately, the decision will be up to you and, since these ladies are your best friends, they'll be happy with whatever dress you select (or at least they'll *say* they are!). While you're out shopping, it's important to adhere to the following two "commandments":

Consider Your Ladies' Body Types: If you plan to have all your bridesmaids wear the same dress, choose a style with structure in a nonclingy fabric (such as cotton, silk dupioni, or taffeta) that will flatter many body types. Another way to accommodate different sizes and shapes is to pick a dress that can be made with a variety of necklines, so each bridesmaid can choose what will look best on her. Lastly, if you trust your ladies' taste, simply provide color and length guidelines and ask each one to choose her own dress style. This works especially well if you're planning to have the bridesmaids wear black.

Be Price Conscious: Keep a price cap in mind and stick to dresses that all your bridesmaids can afford. Again, your friends will be glad to wear what you'd like, so long as it's reasonable. If you're not sure what price is "reasonable," ask your bridesmaids individually what they would be comfortable paying. If you want a dress that exceeds that limit, then make up the difference yourself rather than asking your friends to spend more money.

The groom's outfit

When it comes to choosing the groom's outfit, take into account the venue, the level of formality of the wedding, and, of course, his personality.

As men's formalwear tends to involve more layers than a women's wedding gown, it's also especially important that the season and weather be taken into account when the groom chooses his outfit. While a three-piece tux may look fantastic in a hotel ballroom, it can be downright miserable to wear one at an outdoor wedding on a humid summer's day. Many men opt for a classic lounge suit instead, teamed with a tie or boutonnière that coordinates with the wedding's decorative scheme. For a really casual and informal wedding (on a beach, say, or in your parents' garden), chinos and a nice shirt will do.

Ultimately, the groom should wear an outfit that he feels smart, handsome and comfortable in. A sporty, rugged guy might not be comfortable in white tie and tails, no matter how much you like the look of it. Feel free to make helpful suggestions, but you should leave the final decision up to him (after all, you wouldn't want him dictating what your wedding gown is supposed to look like!).

Q & A

What should I wear to the engagement party, my wedding shower, and the rehearsal dinner?

The formality of engagement parties varies a good deal—you may be holding a formal dinner, in which case a little cocktail dress is in order, or alternatively the celebration could be a low-key brunch or barbecue lunch for which you might don a strappy sundress. A pretty dress or skirt (or designer jeans) and dressy top ensemble would work well for your wedding shower, while the rehearsal dinner affords more of an opportunity to go to town and wear a really beautiful, well-designed dress.

For all of these occasions, you'll want to choose clothes that photograph well, so avoid loud patterns and bulky sweaters or tops that will make you appear heavier in pictures. Also, keep in mind that all your outfits should be family-friendly, meaning something cute and reasonably modest that your grandmother or your fiancé's great-aunt Tilly will approve of too!

I just found out that one of my bridesmaids is pregnant and will be showing at the time of my wedding. What should I do about her dress?

First of all, congratulate your friend—a pregnancy is exciting news that certainly takes precedence over any dress concerns! That said, she should order a dress that's several sizes bigger than her normal size. That way, she'll be able to take the dress to a tailor closer to the wedding date, and they'll have plenty of fabric to work with to fit the dress to her current size.

Some designers also offer bridesmaid dresses in a variety of different silhouettes. If one is available, an empire-line high-waisted dress will be the most comfortable for your friend, and will best disguise her baby bump.

If the dress has already been ordered and the size cannot be changed, the manufacturer should be able to provide additional fabric that your bridesmaid can use to have the dress altered.

family & friends

Choosing your bridesmaids

Deciding on your bridal party may seem an easy task. But there are important factors to take into account before you promise ten of your best friends they can accompany you down the aisle. Take time to consider how many bridesmaids you need and which friends are best suited to the job.

Think of those friends and family members who are your nearest and dearest—the women you've grown up with, laughed with and cried with, who you love best, and who you want surrounding you on this important day of your life—and you'll likely be most of the way towards completing your dream team of bridesmaids. That said, there are a few other factors to consider…

Numbers: Ultimately, when it comes to deciding on the size of your wedding party, you should include as many bridesmaids as will make your wedding day a happier time. Having said that, a dozen ladies lined up alongside the altar leaves few people in the audience if you're having a small wedding

for forty. When choosing how many bridesmaids you want to have, do consider the size of your guest list. If it's on the smaller side, it may work best to ask only your best friend to be your attendant. Also, there's no rule that says there has to be the same number of bridesmaids as groomsmen. Go over your list of potential wedding party members with your fiancé and decide together who will be included. If he wants two attendants and you want four, that's just fine.

The maid of honor: Many people have a relative or best friend eager to step into this honored position. Or you might have two equally important women in your life; in which case, you can count yourself lucky and ask them to share the role. Do be sure to consider the duties that are associated with being maid of honor, and your expectations. If your BF is fun but flakey, it makes sense to make her joint maid of honor with a more practical, organized friend. Alternatively, you could suggest that she enlist the help of your other bridesmaids when it comes to planning the bachelorette/hen party or wedding shower.

Family who expect to be included: When it comes to family who hope to be part of the wedding party, it's generally easier to include them than not. Perhaps you and your sister-in-law-to-be aren't exactly close, for example. However, if she makes it clear that she wants or expects to be a part of the wedding party, unless you have a major concern it's polite to include her. Maybe you'll even bond during the experience. At the very least, you're sure to avoid hearing about how she wasn't included in the wedding on every future holiday.

Friends you're not planning to include: Perhaps you've decided to keep the wedding party on the small side and thus can't include all of your good friends. If you have a girlfriend you don't plan to ask to be a bridesmaid but whose friendship is meaningful to you, let her know how important she is by asking her to get involved in a different way. She might like to give a reading during the ceremony or make a speech at the reception. Friends who have a special talent could even contribute to the wedding in some way that's related to their particular skill.

Friends who don't want to be included: Most likely, everyone you ask will be thrilled and excited to be a part of your wedding. However, if a friend is going through a tough time emotionally, she may not feel up to participating. And if things are tight financially, she may feel unable to shoulder all the expenses that come with being one of the members of the wedding party. Be understanding of people's circumstances.

Other members of the bridal party

Wedding parties come in all sizes and arrangements. When choosing yours, the most important thing is that the ones you love are included.

Ushers: This is a perfect role for family members, male relatives of the bride, or friends you want to include in the bridal party. Traditionally, ushers are men, but nowadays there's no rule to say you can't have female ushers as well. The role of an usher is to greet the guests as they arrive, hand out wedding programs/the order of service, and seat the guests (bride's guests go on the left, groom's on the right) before the ceremony begins. Ushers do not take part in the wedding ceremony, although they may escort parents or grandparents down the aisle during the processional.

Groomsmen: The groomsmen are usually chosen from the groom's best friends or close family members. Traditionally, groomsmen stand up front with the groom both before and during the ceremony, and then accompany the bridesmaids back down the aisle during the recessional.

Flower girls and ring bearers: Children can add to the cute factor of a wedding, so if there are kids that are important to you and your husband-to-be, asking them to be your flower girls or ring bearers is a wonderful gesture. Having more than one little flower girl or ring bearer is fine (in fact, one of each is perfect) and often works better, as it can be a little intimidating for a young child to walk down the aisle alone. Bear in mind that really tiny tots can look adorable all dressed up in their wedding finery, but their behaviour can be unpredictable, so don't expect them to carry out their duties to perfection!

Parents

Naturally, both sets of parents will be a big part of your wedding day. When it comes to determining their roles both during planning and on the big day, look to your relationships for cues as to how to best involve them.

When it comes to parents and weddings, one size most definitely does not fit all! You may choose to have your father or both your parents walk you down the aisle. If you're closer to your mother, you may want her to be your escort. If your fiancé is great friends with his dad, he could be the best man. You can perform a father-daughter dance at the reception or, if you don't enjoy the spotlight, dance together while everyone else is dancing too. The bottom line is that you shouldn't feel pressured to conform to other people's expectations. Focus on being yourself, feeling comfortable, and having fun. The best moments between you and your parents will come naturally.

During the planning process, keeping communication open between you and your fiancé and both sets of your parents is key. In a perfect world, you and your parents' ideas about your wedding, how much it should cost, and who should be invited would fall blissfully into step. But even in the closest families, there's bound to be some differences in opinion. Your parents will look to you and your fiancé to explain how much of a role you'd like them to play. From the start, be straightforward about your wishes. If you are clear about your hopes and expectations, misunderstandings won't creep in, and you'll be able to create the wedding you (and they) hope for.

Parties

Once you're engaged, your family and friends will no doubt want to host parties to celebrate. These events offer perfect opportunities for the bride and groom's families to get to know one another better. Parties leading up to your wedding day might include:

Engagement party

Timing: One to four months after becoming engaged

The engagement party is usually hosted by the parents of the bride, though it can also be hosted by the engaged couple or by a close friend. The time of day and level of formality isn't a given—a celebratory lunch or cocktails at sunset work equally well. The point here is to celebrate the next stage of your relationship with your loved ones and get everyone excited about the upcoming wedding.

Wedding shower

Timing: Four to ten weeks before the wedding

Traditionally the bridesmaids and/or the mother of the bride host a female-only shower for the bride, her friends, and close family members. As some find the girls-only concept a little precious, "Jack and Jill" showers that both men and women attend are also popular. This party is an opportunity to "shower" the engaged couple with gifts. Guests bring gifts such as kitchen gadgets, serveware, and linens to help the couple set up home together.

Bachelorette or hen party

Timing: Anywhere from three days to four months before the wedding

Bachelorette or hen parties are usually planned by the maid of honor and attended by the women in the bridal party as well as other close friends of the bride. These parties can range from a casual dinner at a friend's house or restaurant to a wild three-day party in Las Vegas. Ultimately, what you choose to do should be determined by what

sort of event the bride will most enjoy, but it's also important to bear in mind what the invitees can afford.

Rehearsal dinner

Timing: The night before the wedding

Hosted either by the groom's parents or by the engaged couple, the rehearsal dinner always takes place the evening before the wedding. All the wedding party must be invited, although many couples also choose to open the dinner up to include all their out-of-town guests.

The bride (you) and groom (him)

Everyone will tell you that your engagement will be one of the happiest times of your life, and this is true. However, that doesn't mean there won't be a few little ups and downs along the way…

Adding the time it takes to plan a wedding to two already busy schedules can be exhausting and, frankly, a little stressful.

Bear this in mind, and be sure to keep the lines of communication open and to be honest with one another throughout the planning process. Set specific time aside to discuss the multitude of wedding-related matters that will come up, but also set some time aside to spend together *without* any wedding talk. Modern weddings are largely about expressing your personalities and creating an event that is representative of your relationship, so keep an open mind and know that you can shape your day to be whatever suits the two of you best.

Lastly, try to keep things in perspective. You throw a wedding because you want your friends and family to witness your commitment to each other, and because you want to enjoy a fun, joyous celebration with the ones you love. Just remember that you're getting married because you've found the person you want to share the rest of your life with and, ultimately, this is the most important thing!

Gift ideas for the wedding party

It's customary to give the members of your wedding party a small gift in thanks for being a part of your day. Here are a few easy gift ideas:

wearable	*useful*
Bridesmaid: pashmina or silk scarf; classic pearl earrings	Bridesmaid: personalized stationery or photo frame
Groomsmen/ushers: cufflinks	Groomsmen/ushers: Tool kit; letter opener; monogrammed pocket knife
Flower girl: charm bracelet	Flower girl: Monogrammed sleepover bag or tote bag
Ring bearer: cool pair of sneakers/trainers; watch	Ring bearer: Monogrammed backpack; money box

creative	*fun*
Bridesmaid: pretty journal and nice pen	Bridesmaid: gift certificate for a massage or other beauty treatment
Groomsmen/ushers: beer- or wine making kit	Groomsmen/ushers: movie or sports tickets to watch their team
Flower girl: Face-painting kit or friendship-bracelet-making kit	Flower girl: dress-up box; bridal outfit for a favorite doll
Ring bearer: Model-building kit	Ring bearer: board game or chess set

the wedding day

Creating a wedding day timeline

To help ensure your wedding day runs smoothly, it's helpful to put together a "big day" schedule for everyone involved, especially the photographer. Here's an example of what a wedding day timeline might look like.

11:00am ❊ Brunch with your bridesmaids.

12:30–2:30pm ❊ Hair and makeup for you, your bridesmaids, and your mother. It's nice to give your bridesmaids the option of having their hair and makeup done professionally, if you can afford to treat them.

3:30–4:15pm ❊ Group photos with attendants followed by photos with family.

4:15pm ❊ Guests begin to arrive. Wedding party arrives at the ceremony site.

5:00–5:30pm ❊ Ceremony.

5:30–6:00pm ❊ Guests travel to the reception venue; bride and groom have photos taken.

6:00–7:00pm ❊ Cocktail hour.

7:00–7:15pm ❊ Guests are seated for dinner.

7:15–8:00pm ❊ Toasts are made by the bride's father, best man, and maid of honor. Dinner is served.

8:30pm ❊ Bride and groom's first dance, followed by father-daughter dance.

9:00pm ❊ Cake-cutting.

9:30pm ❊ Band or DJ starts.

11:00pm ❊ Reception ends and bride and groom depart.

The ceremony

Wedding ceremonies vary greatly depending upon the religious beliefs of the bride and groom. You'll work with your officiant to create a ceremony that's meaningful to you both, but here are some ideas to get you started.

Order of processional
This varies according to religious traditions but might look something like this:
Grandparents
Parents of the groom
Mother of the bride
Bridesmaids (alone or escorted by the groomsmen/ushers)
Ring bearers/page boys
Flower girls
(Alternatively, bridesmaids, flower girls and ring bearers may follow the bride down the aisle rather than preceding her.)
Bride (escorted by her father or by both parents)

Popular ceremony readings
I Corinthians 13: 1–13
Song of Solomon 2: 10–13

Ecclesiastes 4: 9–12
"Touched by an Angel," by Maya Angelou
"Poem 43," from *Sonnets from the Portuguese* by Elizabeth Barrett Browning
"The Wedding Prayer," by Robert Louis Stevenson
"The Art of Marriage," by Wilferd Peterson

Music for the prelude and processional
"Jesu, Joy of Man's Desiring," by Bach
"Allegro Maestoso," by Handel
"Air on the G String," by Bach
"Ave Vernum Corpus," by Mozart

Music for the bride's entrance
"Bridal Chorus," by Wagner
"Canon in D," by Pachelbel
"Trumpet Voluntary in D Major," by Clarke
"Ave Maria," by Schubert

Music for the recessional

"The Wedding March," by Mendelssohn
"Hornpipe," by Handel
"March," by Verdi
"Autumn," (from *The Four Seasons*)
by Vivaldi

Sonnet 116 by William Shakespeare

Let me not to the marriage of true minds
Admit impediments. Love is not love
Which alters when it alteration finds,
Or bends with the remover to remove:
O no! it is an ever-fixed mark
That looks on tempests and is never shaken;
It is the star to every wandering bark,
Whose worth's unknown, although his height be taken.
Love's not Time's fool, though rosy lips and cheeks
Within his bending sickle's compass come;
Love alters not with his brief hours and weeks,
But bears it out even to the edge of doom.
If this be error upon me proved,
I never writ, nor no man ever loved.

The reception

The two of you have tied the knot and now it's time to party!

Depending upon the time of your ceremony, there are several types of receptions you may want to consider:

Dinner reception

The seated dinner reception is the most formal and most traditional option. They usually begin between 6:00pm and 7:30pm and include a cocktail hour, followed by dinner and dancing. A more casual variation would be a buffet dinner.

Cocktail reception

A cocktail reception is a good alternative for late afternoon or early morning weddings. They can begin around 5:00pm and go on for two or three hours (your guests head to dinner on their own afterwards). Or, the reception could begin after guests have had dinner (around 8:00pm) and include dancing until 11:00pm or midnight—an option that works well for ceremonies held early in the day. There's no need to serve a meal, but it's a good idea to provide light hors d'oeuvres or a dessert buffet for guests to nibble on.

Brunch or lunch receptions

For weddings between 11:00am and 1:00pm, a brunch or lunch reception offers a way to mingle with guests over a meal that's less expensive than a fancy dinner. Keep it casual: buffet-style works well for an afternoon reception, as do summery drinks. For entertainment you might try old-fashioned lawn games set to the sounds of a small, low-key band or string quartet.

Music for the reception
First-dance songs
"Calico Skies," Paul McCartney
"At Last," Etta James

"Better Together," Jack Johnson
"The Way You Look Tonight," Michael Bublé
"Ain't That Love," Ray Charles
"You Are the Sunshine of My Life," Stevie Wonder

Father-daughter dance songs
"When You Wish Upon a Star," Steve Tyrell and Chris Botti
"Father and Daughter," Paul Simon
"Little Miss Magic," Jimmy Buffett
"Wonderful World," Louis Armstrong

"My Girl," The Temptations
"Daughter," Loudon Wainwright III

Cake-cutting songs
"Baby I Love You," Aretha Franklin
"Signed, Sealed, Delivered (I'm Yours)," Stevie Wonder
"L-O-V-E," Nat King Cole
"Our Love is Here to Stay," Billie Holiday
"I Hear a Symphony," The Supremes
"Can't Get Enough of Your Love, Babe," Barry White

Troubleshooting

Unfortunately "the best laid plans…oft go awry," even on wedding days.

When it comes to your wedding day, you should feel secure in the fact that your wedding professionals will work at dozens of events every year and have contingency plans for most of the problems that might arise on the big day.

However, even if things are going according to plan, questions may arise about when or where things should be delivered and how you want them to be arranged. If you've planned the wedding yourself but don't want to worry about the flowers arriving on time, whether it's time to cut the cake yet, or any last-minute catering challenges on the actual day, you may want to consider hiring a day-of-wedding coordinator. They usually charge by the hour and will make sure that your wedding day runs smoothly from start to finish. Should something unexpected occur, the coordinator will be in charge of handling it and will only come to you with questions if they absolutely have to. Another option is to appoint a levelheaded friend or family member as the point-of-contact person or problem-solver for the day. Hand over all the contact information and go through your wedding day timeline with them so that if something comes up they're ready to step in and resolve any problems.

After you've done all the preparation you can, relax and enjoy the day. Be present in the moment and embrace your wedding for what it is. Come rain or shine, you've just begun a new life with someone you love, and that is truly something to celebrate.

Q & A

If someone has been invited to the wedding shower, do they have to be invited to the wedding?

The short answer is yes. The tradition of a wedding shower implies that guests bring presents to help the new couple stock their home, and it would be incredibly ungrateful to ask a person to come to an event and give a gift, then not invite them to the actual wedding. Generally, the host/hostess of your shower will ask you for a list of people you would like to invite. If you're worried about them inviting additional people, be sure to discuss your concerns with them before the shower invitations are sent out.

I'd rather our reception was adults only. What's the best way to let guests know that children shouldn't attend?

The best way to indicate this is to address your invitations only to the members of a family who are invited. For example, if the Smiths have two young children, you would just address the invitation to Mr. and Mrs. Bob Smith. If people have questions, they will get in touch with you and your fiancé or your families. Most people will understand, but be prepared for the fact that by not inviting children some guests with kids may not be able to attend.

Is it OK to have a cash bar at my reception?

No, not really. Your closest friends and family have come to help celebrate with you and they shouldn't have to pay to have a drink. If you're worried about keeping costs down, you could limit the alcohol available to just beer and wine. Or you could offer an open bar during cocktail hour and switch to wine and beer only after dinner. The long and the short of it is that, unless you're planning a completely dry (alcohol-free) celebration, guests should get to imbibe for free.

Who exactly is supposed to give a toast at the reception?

The father of the bride traditionally offers the first toast as a way of welcoming guests once everyone has been seated for dinner. It's also tradition that the best man will offer a toast at some point during the dinner portion of the reception. It's also increasingly common for the maid of honor to make a toast as well. The speeches don't have to relate to one another, but it's generally the case that the best man's speech will focus on the groom, while the maid of honor's speech will focus on the bride. It's also a nice gesture for the couple to formally address their guests together and thank them for coming—a good time for this is either just after the other speeches, or during the cutting of the cake.

Picture credits